YOU HAVE WHAT THE *Father* HAS

YOU HAVE WHAT THE FATHER HAS

How To Possess The Promises Of The Father

Unless otherwise indicated, Scriptures are taken from the King James Version of the Bible. Unless otherwise indicated, all definitions are taken from Merriam Webster's Online Dictionary.

Printed in the United States of America

ISBN 978-0-9960557-1-0

YOU HAVE WHAT THE *Father* HAS

HOW TO POSSESS THE PROMISES OF THE FATHER

WRITTEN BY:

LYDIA J. NANCE

YOU HAVE WHAT THE *Father* HAS

Dedication

This book is first dedicated to my heavenly Father and Savior, Jesus Christ. Thank you, Father, for your grace and mercy and for helping me mature and grow in you everyday. Thank you for loving me when it felt as though no one else did.

Second, I dedicate this book to my husband, Dr. Steven Nance, who has loved and supported me. Thank you for your love, sacrifice, and encouragement through the many challenges that life brings. I appreciate your strength and character, as well as your consistency in godliness and love for me. Thank you for your patience and for loving me as Christ loves the church.

Next, I dedicate this book to my children (Lamont, Cherrish, Charity, Chyna, and Joy), who I love and appreciate.

You-HAVE-WHAT

THE

Father

HAS

Table of Contents

You-HAVE-WHAT
THE
Father
HAS

Preface

After coming into the revelation of the Father's love for me and why certain elements in my life were missing—such as my identity, self-esteem, and security—a passion was birthed in me to share my struggle, experience, and victory with others who have similar struggles.

To be honest, this book has probably been one of the hardest things I have ever done because of the many emotional changes it has taken me through—not to mention the spiritual battles of the mind I have encountered. Although it has taken some time to write this book, I am thankful for all God has given me to write and his consistent fatherly encouragement, and the process he took me through, for it has truly humbled me and made me wiser and stronger.

My heart aches for many young women as well as men who have not come into a real relationship or the knowledge of the true love of our heavenly Father—they don't know God the Father for themselves. They run from one abusive relationship to another and practice other destructive behaviors trying to fill the void in their lives. Most don't understand their rich inheritance in Christ and the love of the Father, so they walk around in condemnation (the spirit of guilt, shame, and hopelessness). Note: The spirit of condemnation arrests you and prevents you from moving forward to your destiny.

I'm not talking about just knowing the existence of God and the stories heard about how God brought mother, father, or grandmother through hard times, but I am talking about knowing God as heavenly Father for yourself in an intimate way. Once you do that, you are content and empowered. God is Father not just because he is the creator of all things and provider of our needs, but because he is intimately concerned about you and every aspect of your being.

Take a look at what the Scripture says: "Are not two sparrows sold for a penny? Yet not one of them will fall to the ground outside your Father's care. And even the very hairs of your head are all numbered. So don't be afraid; you are worth more than many sparrows." (Matthew 10:29-30 NLT)

God cares so much for you that he sent his only begotten son, Jesus Christ, to redeem you from every curse of sin. As a matter of fact, he loves you so much that he has given you all things, and because Christ died for our redemption, "you have what the Father has" for you. In other words, all that you need and want has already been provided for you through Jesus Christ. You are already healed, delivered, and blessed. Now it's up to you to access it by faith and confidence in his love and faithfulness. It's yours!

I really believe that there will be a healing in your heart and a renewing of your mind as you read the pages of this book. I am confident that you will experience freedom and be empowered by Holy Spirit.

To help you get the full benefit from reading this book, read it from cover to cover and complete each set of Empowerment Tools and meditate on each of the Power Scriptures found at the end of each chapter. You can also pray the prayers in this book. You can pray them exactly as they appear in this book or add to them as Holy Spirit leads you.

The Father has richly blessed you,

Pastor Lydia Nance

You-HAVE-WHAT

THE

Father

HAS

Acknowledgments

I want to acknowledge all my sisters and brothers. My late mother and forever hero (Diane Bryant McClain) and my sister (Syleenia Angela Bryant). How I miss you both. Rest in peace.

To all my family: Thank you for your confidence in me. Because of you, I've been able to write this book.

Finally, to my wonderful ministry family, Philadelphia Outreach Ministries: Thank you for dreaming with me and for your faithfulness and support.

You-HAVE-WHAT
THE
Father
HAS

Introduction

A Painful Flashback of My Past

Tears fell from my eyes as the car my father was in sped off. Part of me wanted him to leave and part of me wanted him to stay. I was eleven years old and did not understand all that was happening. There were so many questions in my little head that I felt dizzy. That moment will be seared into my mind forever.

As I ran behind the car waving goodbye to my father, unbeknownst to me I was waving goodbye to the provision, protection, security, identity, discipline, and much needed love of an earthly father as well. My father had his faults, but as a young girl, I needed him.

My father never returned to our home and growing up without a father was very difficult for me. I watched my mother come home night after night exhausted from cleaning toilets and cafeterias at one of the local elementary schools. She had graduated from high school, but until my father left, she had only worked occasionally outside the home. I remember her screaming for joy when the school district offered her a job as a janitor. She was so happy to be working. We were on welfare and getting a job and having her own paycheck was one of her goals. I also remember her saying she couldn't wait to get off welfare because the people who worked in the social services offices talked to her badly. Moreover, giving very personal information to perfect strangers felt degrading, and her experiences stripped her of her self-worth and dignity. She was a hard worker and instilled the same work ethic in us.

My mother had seven children—five girls and two boys. We lived in a mid-sized house in a close-knit neighborhood that soon went downhill. There were many things for us to get hooked up with—drugs, alcohol, prostitution, gangs—so my mother prayed often and fought to keep us occupied with summer jobs, summer camps, church, and much discipline in the hopes of guiding us to the positive things in life. I can't say that we made all the right choices (I know I made many mistakes), but she always tried to help us. She was wise, kind, loving, strong, and a God-fearing person and lived out a good example before us. My mother loved us deeply and dearly.

No matter how hard my mother tried, however, she could not replace the presence of a father. No mother, no matter how loving and hardworking, can. Despite her best efforts, we still needed a father's protection, provision, discipline, and love. We desperately needed to feel that security that a father provides. Without it, I believe we grew up feeling insecure and constantly trying to prove ourselves, especially to the opposite sex.

My mother felt his absence, too. She was not a big complainer, and her tears were few, at least in front of us. Sometimes I would hear or see her crying and praying in our basement. Perhaps we did not have enough food, or perhaps our electricity or gas was about to be turned off again. There were times we did not have food, and she desperately looked forward to the first of the month when we got our food stamps. I hated going to the store with food stamps because some of the kids would make fun of me, even though I believe they had food stamps as well. Lol. I'm sure there was always a bill to be paid or some other obstacle my mother faced. Nevertheless, we always survived, and even though I was not close to my father, I secretly wished he were there to help us.

As a child, I remember my father coming home late and sometimes making my mother cry. I didn't like that. One winter day, I remember him taking all of us—me, my sisters, and my brothers, along with my mother—for a ride after church in our old station wagon. There was a small lake on our way home, and he started skidding and wildly turning the station wagon, pretending he was going to drive out onto the frozen water. I could see the terror in my mother's eyes as she gripped the handle on the side of the door. I was afraid as well. I was afraid because my mother was afraid. My father would often drive crazy when he was upset. I believe that's why my mother never learned to drive and was always so nervous when she was riding with anyone. But that is just my speculation. These kinds of experiences made me fearful of my father. From it, I learned fear, terror, and distrust. I cannot explain why I remember this event so vividly, but I think it was the horror my mother displayed in her face and the feeling of helplessness I felt.

Although my father instilled fear in me, his absence was just as terrifying. I remember the first day I felt the vulnerability of growing up without him. I was walking over the bridge to go to school with my little sister. We lived upstate New York where it stayed cold. I remember having to walk one mile to get to school every day. I liked walking in the summertime. We were young (I believe about eleven and thirteen years old). There were two mannish boys (as older people say) who lived near us. One of them was much older. As my little sister and I walked over the bridge, they approached us and began to say nasty things, referring to our private body parts. I was afraid, and my first instinct was to protect my little sister. My heart felt as though it were going to pound through my chest. The boys grabbed us. It was very early in the morning, and I didn't see anyone who could help. I told my little sister to run. She ran, and they grabbed me. I wanted to tell them that I was going to tell my father. I wanted to scream for him, but I knew he wasn't there. I began fighting back.

Although they did not rape me, they fondled me, reaching in and under my clothes, and touching me in places I did not give them permission to touch. I could smell alcohol on the breath of the older one, who eventually let me go. I was horrified. I felt violated. I was so traumatized that I had flashbacks about it for months. I was afraid to walk to school. Had it not been broad daylight, I believe they would've done more to me.

I told my mother, and I guess I hoped that they would be arrested. Instead, she talked to me about what happened and instructed me to stay with the other children as I walked to school. It was her way of protecting me, I guess, but I was very upset that nothing else was done. I wanted the boys punished. I felt vulnerable and scared. I felt uncovered and angry. It was at that point I realized I had to fend for myself. No one else was going to defend or take care of me. My mother had her plate full with seven growing children and no one to help her. She lived about three hours away from her immediate family and rarely depended on them for support. She was the oldest and had many sisters and brothers. There were probably twelve or thirteen of them.

My father's absence coupled with the attack had a deep impact on how I felt about myself. It had a deep impact on the choices I made for my life, as well. I grew up angry, passionately independent, and defensive.

After most of us were grown up, my mother eventually married again, and the man she married made her happy. He was a good husband and stepfather. I had never seen her so happy before. The day of her wedding, which was held at The Botanical Gardens in upstate New York, was amazing. She walked in on "Here and Now" by Luther Vandross. She was so beautiful in her pink wedding dress. Her eyes sparkled as she flashed a big smile with her full, pink lips. Tragically, her happiness was short-lived. She was diagnosed with pancreatic cancer and died three years later. On the day she died, my biological father called to ask if she was dead. I was very mean to him and told him that he was not going to get his hands on our house. I thought, "the nerve of him calling at this time." He was the last person I wanted to talk to, but he was probably the first person I needed.

As time went on, and I became a woman, I still carried the mind-set of distrust, insecurity, and super-independence. I secretly harbored hurt and was broken in places that only the Father knew or could heal. I struggled with low self-esteem, who I was, and the genuineness of true love, no matter who it was coming from. I always had to be in control of my feelings and stayed on guard.

Nobody's word was good enough for me. I just knew there was a hidden agenda. I vowed that I would not marry a man like my father, but as life would have it, I did. I married a man who claimed he was a minister. We fell in love and stayed married for one week—yes, one week. We got married on a Saturday, and by the next Saturday, I was calling the lawyer's office after finding out that he had been married twice before and had three children, which he lied about. He turned out to be a pathological liar. He had forged his divorce papers and had been with a woman the night before our wedding day. What's more disappointing, is that the people I trusted knew of his infidelity but didn't tell me until after the wedding.

I was devastated. All my life I had dreamed of getting married and having someone who really loved me. That dream was crushed with a simple "I do" to the wrong person. I had finally trusted someone, and that trust was taken for granted.

After my divorce, my life started spiraling downward. I will not speak of all my past hurts, countless mistakes, and disappointments in this book, but I was on a path to nowhere. I felt no one was genuine and trusted no one. I longed for and needed love so badly. I blamed God for letting bad things happen to me. I now understand that not having a good example of an earthly father or even the concept of who a father truly is, drastically affected my relationship with my heavenly Father. It also affected my other relationships. I struggled with painful questions such as, If God loves me, why didn't he help me? Why couldn't I just have a normal and happy family? Will God really help someone like me?

Please understand that this struggle is real for many people. Both from personal experience and from counseling many hurting people (male, female, young and old), I have found that growing up without a father or with a distant or disconnected father can cause our relationships to suffer more than we realize. It can also affect our relationship with our heavenly Father. There are so many people with this deep hurt who have become adept at hiding this reality but have never truly healed, because they have effectively covered and bandaged their hurts. Please know that if you don't have true healing, the hurt will eventually reveal itself.

I believe there are many people, especially those who have been hurt, wounded, and disappointed, who live their lives as self-reliant individuals because self-reliance is how they have survived. Handling matters on their own is the way they know and trust. As a result, they forfeit the blessed assurance of truly knowing and having a relationship with the one who created them, who loves them, and whom they can count on the most—God the Father.

Even though we may not consciously realize it, when we have been hurt, we can develop the destructive attitude of super independence. But God wants us to depend on and trust Him as Father. He wants us to lean on Him. Jesus prayed often to the Father. He is our example.

Our heavenly Father wants the best for us, and that is why he gave us his best, Jesus Christ.

Regardless of what type of father you had growing up and regardless of your past experiences and hurts, the Father wants you to experience his unconditional love. He displayed that love when he gave you Jesus Christ. He wants you to fulfill your purpose, no matter how rough your road has been in getting there. He wants you to achieve your goals, feel secure in him, and live your dreams and "the good life."

The Father is equipped and more than prepared for your future. He doesn't need to start a savings plan to take care of you. He has no need of nothing, and his resources are unlimited. He wants the very best for you, even more than you may understand.

If there is something missing or broken in your life, he wants to fill that void and bind up all the broken pieces. If you have a need, he wants to meet it. He wants to be your provider. The Father longs to hear from you and give you your heart's desires. Don't miss out on all that our heavenly Father has for you by going through life as though you are fatherless. You can have what the Father has for you. He has given you everything you need.

Chapter 1

What Does "You Have What the Father Has" Really Mean?

You have what the Father has for you. Do you believe that? We can say we believe it, but do we really? Do we really trust our heavenly Father? One night while I was praying at our midweek service, God put in my spirit to declare that I have what the Father has! At the time I didn't understand what I was declaring until God revealed to me that all that I am praying for already belongs to me by faith. Now understand that this didn't mean that I shouldn't pray but that I should pray from a place of faith in KNOWING or having the revelation that God has it in his will and plan for me to possess all that he has provided for me. Please know that I'm not just talking about physical things, but spiritual healing (emotionally, physically, and spiritually), spiritual understanding and growth, deliverance, freedom, peace, and financial well-being. You see we don't have to beg our heavenly Father for anything. He takes pleasure in blessing us. There are so many things the Father has given us that we are not fully aware of or have not received. So, when I say that "You have what the Father has," I want you to understand that Christ has given you all you need to live life abundantly. However, it's up to you to believe it, receive it, and possess it!

As a little girl, I was always curious about what my parents possessed in their bedroom. It was a secret place to me. In those days, parents did not allow children in their bedrooms and kept this part of the house off-limits. At least, that is the way it was in our house.

Every opportunity I had, I would sneak in and go through their personal belongings. I soon became very familiar with what was in that "secret place." I knew where my mother kept her favorite perfume and what kind of jewelry she had. I knew where my father hid his pocket change and comic books.

Just as a child is naturally curious about what is in his or her parents' bedroom, those who belong to Jesus Christ should be curious about what our heavenly Father has for them as well. But unlike the secrets in our parents' bedrooms, the wonderful and fascinating riches of our Father are not only ours to discover, but also to possess and keep. He gladly welcomes us into his secret place, and he encourages us to seek his kingdom and all his righteousness (Matthew 6:33). Our Father is rich and has many treasures for us to seek out and possess. Let's look at the scripture below:

And I will give you treasures hidden in the darkness—secret riches. I will do this so you may know that I am the LORD, the God of Israel, the one who calls you by name. (Isaiah 45:3)

Too often, our view of God the Father has been distorted by false teaching and past experiences. It is time to revolutionize the way you view God as Father. He loves you and is concerned about you as his child. He has prepared the way for you as his beloved.

"I decree and declare that you will renew your mind and upgrade your thinking to come out of the dungeon of life and live in the palace of your heavenly Father."

As you read this book, I pray that you will claim your birthright as a believer and come to know and accept your true identity and take what is rightfully yours. I pray that you come into the knowledge of your rights as a child of God through Jesus Christ, who sits on the right-hand side of the Father and has declared that all things are yours (1 Corinthians 3:21-22). It is my prayer that you will discover the true heart of the Father concerning you. As you read, I decree and declare that you will receive healing and a rededicated heart. I decree and declare that you will renew your mind and upgrade your thinking to come out of the dungeon of life and live in the palace of your heavenly Father.

When you finish this book, I believe that you will no longer doubt that you deserve the best or hesitate to receive the goodness of God through unbelief, low self-esteem, or doubt. Holy Spirit will show you the spiritual rooms filled with all that you need and desire. It is our inheritance, reserved in heaven for us for eternity.

Know Your Inheritance!

Before we can possess our inheritance, we must know what we have inherited. We need to know what the Father has given us through Christ Jesus. What are some of those riches and wonders that God has reserved for us?

Eternal Life

Salvation is a gift by the grace of God, and you cannot work for it. It is not something you earn. It is a gift you receive. When you die, you will forever live with God the Father. By accepting Jesus Christ as the sacrifice on the cross for your sins, you were put in right relationship with God and given eternal life.

For God loved the world so much that he gave his one and only Son, so that everyone who believes in him will not perish but have eternal life. God sent his Son into the world not to judge the world, but to save the world through him. There is no judgment against anyone who believes in him. But anyone who does not believe in him has already been judged for not believing in God's one and only Son. (John 3:16-18 NLT)

1. Sonship

Even if you feel alone or abandoned in this world, if you have accepted Jesus as your Lord and Savior, know that you are part of a new family now—God's family. You have been adopted. You are born again, a newly begotten child of God. This is an eternal family, the family of God.

"So you are no longer strangers and outsiders. You are citizens together with God's people. You are members of God's family." (Ephesians 2:19 NIV)

As part of God's family, you are no longer alone. You have a great family, the body of Christ. There are many who feel alone and alienated, even in the church. That is why my husband and I stress to our members the importance of making people feel a part of our ministry. We have inside greeters whose primary role is to reach out to visitors and new attendees every time we meet for service. Our ministry teaches people how to spiritually restore anyone, whether new to the congregation or not. Our goal is to let people know that they are loved because God is love, and they are family.

"As part of God's family, you are no longer alone. You have a great family, the body of Christ."

Family is the most important support structure one could have as it offers belonging, acceptance, recognition, and identity. Even if your earthly family structure is broken—if you were hurt, abandoned, or rejected—you are loved as a member of God's family. Even if one or more of your parents is in jail, deceased, or no longer in the picture, God's family is secure around you. Even if your children do not speak to you or if you feel as though you've let them down, you are accepted in the family of God. No matter what your family looks like here on earth, you are a part of God's perfect, intact family because you are in Christ.

2. Unconditional Love and Acceptance

You have the Father's unconditional love and acceptance. Nothing in heaven or on earth can separate you from that love (Romans 8:38-39). In Christ, we have unconditional love and acceptance that we cannot lose. You have belonging and security!

3. Power and Authority

Our heavenly Father has given us the power and ability to overcome every difficulty we face in life. He has also given us authority over the enemy (the devil) to bind or stop him from oppressing us. To oppress means, to afflict or torment, to lie heavy on (the mind, imagination), and to overwhelm. Thank God we have been given the authority in Jesus' name to stand against him.

The devil belongs under your feet, and you have the right to put him there with the power and authority God has given you through Jesus Christ, Jesus has been given all power in heaven and earth by the Father (Matthew 28:18), and we have power through him.

Let's look at Luke 10:19 (AMP), which says, "Behold! I have given you authority and power to trample upon serpents and scorpions, and [physical and mental strength and ability] over all the power that the enemy [possesses]; and nothing shall in any way harm you." Hallelujah!

4. Faith and Confidence

That's right. God has given every man the measure of faith (Romans 12:3). It has been given to us, and our responsibility is to use it and operate in it.

A side benefit of faith is confidence. The more you come to understand your position and who you are as a child of God, the more you will gain confidence as never before. Once you realize your rights as a child of God, you will no longer walk in fear or rejection again. Let's look at this promise in the Bible: "We are confident that he hears us whenever we ask for anything that pleases him. And since we know he hears us when we make our requests, we also know that he will give us what we ask for" (1 John 4:14-15). How powerful is that? Beloved, meditate on this Scripture so it is deeply embedded in your heart and watch doors open for you!

Erase the notion that you are not entitled to God's best because of your background, race, or family skeletons, or because of your current place in life or any place from which you've come. Many Christians forfeit kingdom living, the abundance of the glory, and love of God through lack of faith, knowledge, understanding, and confidence in what Jesus has done in bringing us into right relationship with the Father.

5. Access to the Covenant Promises

The Bible is full of God's covenant promises and God is faithful to his Word. Now that you have accepted Jesus Christ by faith (or at the time that you choose to do so), you have full access to them. Included in those promises are your wealth, health, and success. After all, a promise is a promise, and God is faithful to his Word as we understand from the Scripture where God kept His covenant promise that Abraham would have a son in his old age.

"The LORD kept his word and did for Sarah exactly what he had promised. [2] She became pregnant, and she gave birth to a son for Abraham in his old age. This happened at just the time God had said it would. [3]And Abraham named their son Isaac." (Genesis 21:1-3)

Now, please pray this prayer:

Heavenly Father, I acknowledge you as Father. I claim my right to my inheritance through Christ, who has brought me into right relationship with you. I will no longer walk in fear, guilt, or condemnation. I will walk in faith and confidence as your child. I know, Father, that I can depend on you in every area of my life. I am grateful, Father, that I have access to every promise for me in your Word as your dear child. Thank you for opening your rich treasures to me.

Empowerment Tools

Write down the five benefits of being a loved and accepted member of the family of God listed in this chapter. Use the lines below to write down each one and what it means to you.

1.

2.

3.

4.

5.

Power Scriptures

John 1:12

But to all who believed him and accepted him, he gave the right to become children of God.

Ephesians 1:4-5

Even before he made the world, God loved us and chose us in Christ to be holy and without fault in his eyes. 5 God decided in advance to adopt us into his own family by bringing us to himself through Jesus Christ. This is what he wanted to do, and it gave him great pleasure.

Chapter 2

Father, Father

When we think of a father, we think of someone who is a loving protector, pillar of strength, supporter, disciplinarian and encourager. He's an example to his daughter on how she should be treated by her husband. He shows her that nothing is too good for her and that she is beautiful and worthy of the best. A father teaches his son how to be strong, responsible, respectful of others, and a man of integrity. He shows his son how to treat his wife and provide for his family. We think of a father as one who teaches his children about values. He encourages them throughout life, providing guidance, sound advice, and discipline when necessary.

Our heavenly Father is the ideal father and fulfills all these roles perfectly. He is the originator and inventor of fatherhood. He is the giver of all life. He had you in mind before the foundation of the world, and he still does. He is the lover of your soul. He is the Alpha and Omega. In him is your beginning and end. He is the Father who loves you so much that he gave his only begotten Son, Jesus. In Him, you have your true identity. You were made in his likeness and his image. You were made to be victorious in every situation. He is the one who called you to live on top of the world and not be crushed beneath it. He is the provider, not only for you, but for the entire world. He has the whole world in His hands!

From the Scriptures we know that Jesus knew the Father and the Father knew him. Jesus prayed often to God and spent time with him. Jesus always heard from God and performed miracles. Jesus accepted his assignment from God and fulfilled his purpose on the cross, tearing down everything that separated us and bringing us near to God. Hallelujah!

From the time my daughter was born, I have often observed the tender relationship between a father and his child. When my husband taught our daughter to ride a bike, he held up the bike and coached her along the way. She would pedal along on the sidewalk, wobbling slightly from side to side. Eventually he would let her go, and she would rock and reel. When it looked as though she were going to fall, he would grab the handles or the seat and stabilize it. One day I stood there crying, realizing she was crossing another milestone in her life and thanking God for the blessing of a father to walk with her along the way. She was confident that her daddy had her best interest at heart and would not let her fall. She trusted him, so she gladly accepted his instructions. Her father saw the potential in her, so he nurtured that potential until it blossomed. Soon she was riding her bike like a pro and bugging me every day to allow her to do so.

In the same way, our heavenly Father desires to guide us through life and nurture our potential, coaching us through every problem and circumstance by Holy Spirit. Every good father wants the best for his children, and our heavenly Father is better than any earthly father could be.

What stops many of us from knowing God as Father and accepting the coaching and nurturing of our heavenly Father? It is often what I call a "veil mentality." We approach God as though he is concealed or unapproachable as in the days of old. Before the sacrificing of Jesus Christ, you could not approach (come into God's presence) because of your imperfections and blemishes. In those times, a heavy tapestry (or veil) separated the people from the holiest place inside the temple where God dwelt. It was a sacred place, and only one priest could enter it once a year. But when Jesus died on the cross, that veil ripped from top to bottom. It was God's dramatic way of saying that this separation no longer existed. In Christ, we can now "boldly approach the throne of grace" (Hebrews 4:16), crawling into God's lap and calling him "Abba, Father" (Romans 8:15). He is not just our Father. He is our Daddy (expressing our close intimate relationship with Him).

The ripping of the veil showed us that the separation that once existed between us and God, our heavenly Father, has been removed. When we approach God, it should be in confidence and faith, not with a sense of distance and doubt.

Remember when Philip asked Jesus to show him the Father? Jesus replied that if Philip had seen him, he had seen the Father, who is no longer hidden or distant (John 14:8-9). I believe that Philip had not completely grasped the concept that the Father is one with Jesus and we are one with the Father in Christ Jesus. He still needed proof. He wanted to see instead of believing. Although we have not physically seen Jesus as Philip had, we believe and have experienced and do experience the "proof" of his presence. As believers, Jesus lives in us, giving us the privileged access and oneness with the Father.

When we approach God, it should be in confidence and faith, not with a sense of distance and doubt.

Unfortunately, instead of running to God as a loving father, knowing that his arms are open and ready to receive us, many approach him with a sense of fear, distance, and doubt. They approach him as if the veil were still there. I realize that we all have unique ways of praying, but our prayers should be in confidence and faith, as children, accepted and loved. We should pray not as beggars, but as believers.

God wants to give us the desires of our hearts. This promise is written in his Word and is granted as we delight ourselves in him. "Take delight in the Lord, and he will give you your heart's desires" (Psalm 37:4). Does this mean we get everything we want? No. As a wise and loving Father, God ensures that we only get what is best for us. Isn't this what a loving parent does? A loving parent desires to give his or her children the best but knows that not every request is in the child's best interest. Once we understand and receive God's love, our mind-set begins to change. As we get to know the Father, we allow him to change and mold our hearts and begin to pray according to his will. We begin to ask for those things that are within his will—those things that bring him glory and praise. God wants you to have a new house, new car, children, money in the bank, and overall prosperity, but what's most important is our spiritual wholeness and prosperity first. God wants us healed, delivered, and set free from sin, guilt, and shame. "Seek the kingdom of God above all else, and live righteously, and he will give you everything you need" (Matthew 6:33).

Please know, child of God, that you can approach the Father through Christ with your faults, shortcomings, and imperfections, as well as your needs, for he loves you perfectly. Religion tells you that you can't pray to God or that you must "get right first," but let me make this clear for you—you can approach the Father if you are a drunk, prostitute, drug addict, pimp, thief or whatever other vice or sin you are in and receive forgiveness, salvation, grace, and mercy through Christ Jesus. How else are you to get free from sin but to believe and receive Christ and ASK God our Father to save you? It's already done, and you have what the Father has for YOU. Only believe.

Let's look at this promise in the Word of God. In

John 16:25-28 (MSG), Jesus says, "I've used figures of speech in telling you these things. Soon I'll drop the figures and tell you about the Father in plain language. Then you can make your requests directly to him in relation to this life I've revealed to you. I won't continue making requests of the Father on your behalf. I won't need to. Because you've gone out on a limb, committed yourselves to love and trust in me, believing I came directly from the Father, the Father loves you directly. First, I left the Father and arrived in the world; now I leave the world and travel to the Father."

That is powerful! The Father tenderly loves you. As a born-again believer in Jesus Christ, you can ask him directly and without reservation about anything or for anything. I believe it grieves the heart of God when we are in his presence but doubt his love and provision and stay at a fearful and faithless distance.

Don't Doubt His Love

A young lady I had mentored since youth had gone off to college. When she returned, my husband and I took her out to eat and noticed her attitude of distance. This really bothered me because she is like a daughter to us. I later called her to see what was wrong. She eventually said that while she was away, she had done some things she was not proud of. My initial reaction was one of disappointment. It was not because of what she had done, but because she felt she could not talk to us and did not trust our love for her. She feared we would not view her the same way or perhaps that our love would change. Sure, we wanted her to do right, but our love for her was of a heart and mind to restore her and confirm our love. This is the love and much more that the Father feels for us. We were made righteous (in right standing) and have nothing to fear. God wants us to approach him no matter how difficult our lives or what we have done.

None of us can come into God's presence in our own righteousness. We can enter only because of what Christ has done for us. He made us righteous. Jesus has torn down everything that once separated us from God. When we are in Christ, we can come boldly to the Father without reservation. You have a father in God.

Dismantle Self-Rejection

In over twenty years of ministry, God has graced me with the opportunity and ability to counsel and encourage women and young girls who have been raped, molested, abused, rejected, and mistreated. Many of them have come from dysfunctional homes and have had very difficult lives. Through this, I have learned that one of the primary reasons people don't come to Christ or are not able to receive what the Father has for them is because they feel they are not good enough. They blame and reject themselves for what they have experienced, whether it was in or beyond their control or not. They feel they have done too much wrong. They cannot imagine themselves being new creations and doing good. They have been told over and over again that they are nothing. They have been beaten down with words and actions so that they reject themselves as well as Christ.

How sad! In believing this lie, they forfeit a life of freedom, love, and abundance because of the wrong mind-set given to them by their abusers, the self-righteous, and the world.

I want to dismantle the spirit of rejection now, in the name of Jesus!

Stop trying to fit into the beloved and just know that you are in the beloved. In other words, you are already treasured and unconditionally loved by the Father. When you accepted and chose to trust Christ as your Lord and Savior, you were transferred into the kingdom of God and became an adored member of his family. "Beloved" is a person who is loved much. You are much loved by the Father. Let's look at the following passage of Scripture to reinforce and transform your thinking of being the Father's beloved even the more.

"When Jesus therefore had received the vinegar, he said, 'It is finished': and he bowed his head and gave up the ghost." (John 19:30)

When Jesus died on the cross, he said, "It is finished." The reason that he had come was now complete. Jesus saved us and redeemed us, putting us into right relationship with our heavenly Father. When he died, the work of our salvation was complete. There is nothing more to be done. Having accepted Christ and his redemptive work, we are now the beloved of the Father, saved from sin forever. "People are counted as righteous, not because of their work, but because of their faith in God who forgives sinners" (Romans 4:5). In the Bible,

David said: "Oh, what joy for those whose disobedience is forgiven, whose sins are put out of sight. Yes, what joy for those whose record the Lord has cleared of sin." (Psalm 32:1)

In talking to people about Jesus Christ, I have found many who say, "I need to get myself together before I accept Jesus" or "I need to get right with God first," although their life is in shambles, and they are on the brink of destruction. There is nothing anybody can do to get ready before accepting Jesus. He loves you just the way you are, and his work of salvation is for you even if you are a prostitute, pimp, murderer, gay, lesbian, abused, or a victim of rape or molestation.

Even after you are saved, there is nothing you can do to get more saved. You may need victory over certain areas in your life (fornication, drinking, smoking, adultery, stealing, and the like), but this does not mean you are not saved, but you do need deliverance. The Father has not given us salvation only to take it away when we are struggling to overcome a weakness or suffer from lack of self-discipline. We will, however, pay the consequences of the sin. For example, if I have not obtained victory over stealing and I go to the shopping mall and steal something, I may get caught and go to jail, but this does not mean I'm not saved. I will pay the consequence for my wrongdoing.

Your record has been cleared, according to the Bible, and your sins are no more (Hebrews 8: 10-12). The more we get to know the heavenly Father, the less we will want to sin. As our love for the Father grows, our sinful desires will leave. For example, even after accepting Christ, I used to smoke cigarettes (Newport 100's) and party in nightclubs. I knew I was saved with all my heart, but I still did things I knew God didn't want me to do. Once I received God's truth in his Word about my temple (my body), I began to desire to please God more than myself. I no longer wanted to smoke or party. I quit partying, but I was addicted to cigarettes. One Sunday, the Lord delivered me of cigarette addiction after hearing his Word in church. He took the taste out of my mouth just as I believe that as we learn of him, he takes the taste (or desire) for sin out of our lives. He is the true sanctifier! I have learned that words of condemnation and put-down do not make people stop sinning or operating in the flesh. It is the love of God and his truth that really make them free. I want you to take a moment and meditate on the fact that you are loved by the Father.

From this day forward, declare that you are loved by the Father and you are free from self-rejection and condemnation. Go on, say it out loud!

Empowerment Tools

Have you been reluctant to open your heart to God or ask Him for guidance or to meet a need because you feel unworthy or undeserving? God's love is unconditional and not based on what we feel our worth is. He will give you guidance and instruction daily as well as supply your needs. He will even give you the desires of your heart.

List five reasons you know that God the Father loves you. It can be as simple as, "He woke me up this morning."

1.

2.

3.

4.

5.

Now list five things you need guidance on or need from the Father. Then thank him for them in faith.

1.

2.

3.

4.

5.

Power Scriptures

Philippians 4:19

And this same God who takes care of me will supply all your needs from his glorious riches, which have been given to us in Christ Jesus.

Psalm 37:4

Take delight in the LORD, and he will give you your heart's desires.

Ephesians 3:19

May you experience the love of Christ, though it is too great to fully understand. Then you will be made complete with all the fullness of life and power that comes from God.

Chapter 3

Overcoming Your Identity Crisis

Man is a tri-part being—spirit, soul, and body. Although you are a human being in flesh and body, you are more spirit than you are flesh, according to the Word of God.

You were made in the image of God. God is spirit, and because he created you in his image, you are spirit. When you die, your body will go back to the earth from which it came, but your spirit will live forever. This is important for us to know because when God blesses us, he does so spiritually first.

"Then God said, 'Let us make human beings in our image, to be like us. They will reign over the fish in the sea, the birds in the sky, the livestock, all the wild animals on the earth, and the small animals that scurry along the ground.' So God created human beings in his own image. In the image of God he created them; male and female he created them." (Gen. 1:26-27)

There is an identity crisis that exists in the body of Christ today. I believe this crisis exists because we cannot fathom that we are really royalty or that we are truly the beloved of the Father, who has given us all things. We have been through so much, have been oppressed by the enemy for so long, and heard so many condemning scriptural messages of hell and damnation rather than the grace of God that we reject the very notion of true redemption, acceptance, and adoption into the family of the Highest.

I believe this crisis exists because we cannot fathom that we are really royalty or that we are truly the beloved of the Father, who has given us all things.

Although we are saved and the Bible tells us that we are a royal priesthood and a chosen generation, many of us still do not identify ourselves as citizens of the kingdom of God nor as heirs and joint heirs. We say we are, but do we truly believe it? If we do, why is it not manifested in our daily thoughts and actions? Our understanding is limited and devoid of who we are in Christ. When we are quick to embrace the world's view of us, we are not stable in our identity. We are bombarded with images of this world and what the world says about us. Those images stick in our minds. They stay with us subconsciously, and we cannot see or receive beyond what we think. That identity is burned into us, and what we do and how we think is governed by those worldly images.

Napoleon Hill talks of the subconscious mind

through what he calls "auto suggestion." He wrote: "Auto suggestion is a term which applies to all suggestions and all self- administered stimuli which reach one's mind through the five senses. Stated in another way, auto suggestion is self- suggestion."[1] In layman's terms, Napoleon Hill is saying that as certain images and thoughts enter our minds (images that can be either positive or negative), they influence our thoughts, actions, and perception of ourselves, whether we want them to or not. Or as the Bible says, "For as he thinketh in his heart, so is he." (Prov. 23:7 KJV)

It is our duty to know who and whose we are. We are children of our heavenly Father.

If we don't know who we are or what to do with who we are, we have an identity crisis. We must identify ourselves with our heavenly Father and who he says we are. We must understand that we were made in his image and likeness. Do you see yourself as an ordinary person with no real purpose in life or do you see yourself as a blood-washed, born-again believer who is a joint heir with Christ with a purpose and assignment? The Father sees us as beloved joint heirs with Christ Jesus—and so should we! He sees us as victorious through Christ Jesus, according to His Word. He sees us as who He has made us and for what purpose. Stop identifying yourself with who the devil, the world and negative people around you say you are. Stop identifying yourself with what you have done in the past. The past is the past.

If you have repented and are born again, you have a new identity. Start renewing your mind today by seeing a "new you" with a new identity in Christ through God's Word. Cast down the old imaginations and start transforming your mind.

"For the weapons of our warfare are not carnal, but mighty through God to the pulling down of strong holds;) casting down imaginations, and every high thing that exalteth itself against the knowledge of God and bringing into captivity every thought to the obedience of Christ." 2 Corinthians 10:4-5 KJV

After my divorce, my mind was riddled with negative thoughts. I saw myself as a failure because my marriage had failed, even though I was only married a week. I became depressed, obsessing over the fact that I had only wanted to be married once and wanted it to be perfect. When my marriage ended, something was taken from me that I could never get back. I cannot explain the shame and guilt I carried. Even people in the church looked down at me, saying, "Saved people don't divorce." I wondered if they were right and resigned from the church. What's more, because my ex-husband was a minister, the congregation viewed me as the culprit, even though he had told me he had no children when he had three of them and had been with a woman the night before our wedding. Time will not allow me to tell you all the lies he told.

I was spiritually wounded, utterly devastated, and broken. I carried condemnation, guilt, and shame everywhere I went. It wasn't until God the Father through Holy Spirit comforted me in telling me how much he loved me and who I was that I started seeing myself as victorious! The Father gave me glimpses of being married again and of preaching and teaching the Word of God. He will do the same for you. He will give you a vision of victory and a brand-new life. As I read and meditated on his Word and applied real truth to my life, I start seeing myself as a new creation. This allowed me to cast down those evil imaginations about myself given to me by the devil. I was able to release my past and embrace my future—and you can do the same today!

"Therefore, if any man be in Christ, he is a new creature: old things are passed away; behold, all things are become new. And all things are of God, who hath reconciled us to himself by Jesus Christ, and hath given to us the ministry of reconciliation." (2 Corinthians 5:17-18 KJV)

Do you want to change how you see yourself? Do you want to see yourself as a new creation? If so, then make this confession part of your daily meditation. Say this confession out loud, according to 2 Corinthians 5:17-18:

> *Father, I thank you that I am a new creation according to your Word. The wicked things of my past are now passed away. I have a new beginning, and this is a new day in my life! Thank you, Father*

God, for a fresh promise in my life. Christ has made me right with you. I am your beloved. I am no longer ashamed. I now have a new identity and a new attitude. I will let others know how you transformed my life and are able to transform theirs.

Taking It Further

Let's go a little further in understanding how to overcome the identity crisis.

To overcome an identity crisis, you first must identify yourself with who the Word of God says you are. Please look at this powerful Scripture in Ephesians 1:3-5:

> All praise to God, the Father of our Lord Jesus Christ, who has blessed us with every spiritual blessing in the heavenly realms because we are united with Christ. 4 Even before he made the world, God loved us and chose us in Christ to be holy and without fault in his eyes. 5 God decided in advance to adopt us into his own family by bringing us to himself through Jesus Christ. This is what he wanted to do, and it gave him great pleasure.

In reading this Scripture, the Word of God declares the following about us:

1. *We are blessed with all spiritual blessings because of Christ.*

2. *We are loved, chosen, made righteous, and accepted by Father God.*

3. *We are members of the body of Christ. (That means you are family!)*

4. *We are the apple of his eye. (That means you are loved unconditionally.)*

5. *We are purposed. (That means you have a purpose and assignment from God.)*

God decided in advance to adopt us into his family by bringing us to him through Jesus Christ. The Father is glad that you are his, and the very thought of you gives him pleasure (Ephesians 1:4-5). This further assures me that my heavenly Father loved me long before I knew I was loved, that he chose me, and that I am a part of his family. If you are saved by the grace of God, you have been adopted into the same family. Just as you have a natural family that you love and can identify with, so you also have a spiritual family that you can love and identify with. I encourage you to meditate on these passages of Scripture daily until you can see yourself as one who is blessed in God's family.

You Are One with God

"For we are members of his body, of his flesh, and

of his bones. For this cause shall a man leave his father and mother, and shall be joined unto his wife, and they two shall be one flesh. This is a great mystery: but I speak concerning Christ and the church." (Ephesians 5:30-32) If you are born again, you are one with the Father. What is this "oneness" in God?

Jesus prayed to the Father that we would choose to accept this oneness with him.

When you are one with someone, you are an essential part of that person. A husband and wife are a good example. Spiritually, they are one and they are in covenant. For example, my husband and I sometimes think alike, we often finish each other sentences and sometimes we act alike. We have established life together. We own our cars, houses, bank accounts, and land together as a married couple. We each possess and have rights to what the other possesses, and we share the same last name. We share power and authority together over what belongs to us. His house is my house (or shall I say houses) and his money is my money and vice versa. All that is mine is his and vice versa. God created the covenant of marriage to help illustrate our oneness with him in a way we can understand. "I pray that they will all be one, just as you and I are one—as you are in me, Father, and I am in you. And may they be in us so that the world will believe you sent me. I have given them the glory you gave me, so they may be one as we are one. [23] I am in them and you are in me. May they experience such perfect unity that the world will know that you sent me and that you love them as much as you love me." (John 17:21-23)

I find this particular passage of Scripture to be overwhelmingly powerful. Human words alone cannot express the depth of what they are saying and the rights and privileges they convey to us. I'm lost for words to describe the love and hope they contain. You can have an intimate relationship with the Father because of what Jesus has done through his blood. You can talk to him, and he will respond. You can be in need, and he will supply your need.

You can have an intimate relationship with the Father because of what Jesus has done through his blood.

What It Means for You

We know that we are one with God (John 17:21-23). Understanding this will strengthen your confidence about possessing all that he has for you. As we grow in the knowledge of oneness with the heavenly Father, our will begins to align with his will. Our agenda becomes his agenda. Being one with him is to become more Christ-like. As believers, we cannot do anything without God.

Acknowledge your oneness with Christ today. Pray this prayer:

> *Father, I thank you that I am one with you through Jesus Christ. I acknowledge that I cannot do anything without you. I am a disciple of Jesus Christ and desire to bring glory to you in Jesus' name. Amen.*

Empowerment Tools

Write down five lies that Satan has been telling you concerning who you are. To write them is to confront them. Once you confront these lies and choose God's truth instead, never identify yourself with these lies again. Receive God's truth, love, and acceptance, then cross out this section on this page.

1.

2.

3.

4.

5.

Now write down five truths of who you are in Christ that you learned from this chapter. Start seeing yourself as the Father sees you according to his Word. Perhaps he has been telling you all along, but it's difficult for you to receive.

Receive it now!

1.

2.

3.

4.

5.

Power Scriptures

2 Corinthians 5:17-18

This means that anyone who belongs to Christ has become a new person. The old life is gone; a new life has begun! And all of this is a gift from God, who brought us back to himself through Christ. And God has given us this task of reconciling people to him.

Romans 4:7-8

Oh, what joy for those whose disobedience is forgiven, whose sins are put out of sight. Yes, what joy for those whose record the Lord has cleared of sin.

Chapter 4

(The Master Plan) for the Real You!

From the moment you were born, God had a plan for your life. He carefully crafted one just for you. He predestined you and mapped out each stage of your life. God the Father has predestined you for greatness. He has prepared the way and given you all you need to survive and to be successful. He has empowered you with all that you need to fulfill your dreams and purpose. Embrace His plan for your life now.

"For I know the plans I have for you," says the LORD. "They are plans for good and not for disaster, to give you a future and a hope." (Jeremiah 29:11)

The Father's plan for your life is not like anyone else's. He has crafted it uniquely for you. The new you—the real you—is not like anyone else. Your role in God's kingdom is designed just for you.

You may feel that you have failed miserably. You may feel that you do not measure up to other peoples' expectations or that you are not someone God the Father would use. But God sees you differently. He sees you as a conqueror and overcomer. His love and plan for you have not changed because of how you view yourself or the shame and guilt you carry from the past. Take courage and let the real you come forth. The real you—your born-again spirit— was made to rule and reign. Allow the real you to stand up inside of you. The real you is in Christ, the hope of glory. He resides in you through his Spirit.

Because we have become so used to our flesh and the world in which we live, many of us are not yet acquainted with this new identity given to us by the Father through Christ. The real you is what your heavenly Father says about you. But for that to make a difference in your life, you have to believe it!

Allow the real you to stand up inside of you. The real you is in Christ, the hope of glory. He resides in you through his Spirit.

What goals, ideas, plans, or dreams have you set aside or simply given up on because of a negative mind-set or lack of understanding of what Christ has done to bring you into right relationship with the Father? When we get off the course the Father has prepared, we feel overwhelmed, unfulfilled, unsuccessful, worthless, untalented, and lost. We wander aimlessly, not knowing who we are or what we should be doing. Many of us die with the gift of God still in us unwrapped—all because we never knew our Father and the plan he had determined for us.

This is a sad but true story of a young woman I once knew and whom I once secretly admired. To me she was super talented and full of potential. She was a genius and overflowing with great ideas that she eventually executed into a successful business. I believe with all my heart that one of her ideas was a million-dollar idea. Sadly, she could not overcome self-rejection, low self-esteem, unforgiveness, and lack of self-love. There was a deep bitterness inside her. Under the pressure of emotional pain, sickness, and self- disdain, she chose a life of drugs, promiscuity, and isolation until her death. Things didn't have to end that way. God had great plans for her if she only had accepted his love and discipline. Instead, she fell into the trap set by the devil to take her life. If only she had believed the truth that she was a treasured jewel in the body of Christ. I was grieved and angry at her death because there had been a gift of contribution in her, not only for her family but for the body of Christ and the world. That gift died with her.

You, too, have a destiny and contribution to make. Don't give up. Let the real you come shining through and fulfill God's plan for you.

It's Never Too Late

It doesn't matter where we are in life or where circumstances have taken us. It is never too late to embrace the real you. The real you is destined for purpose, and you have a contribution to make to the world.

In the words of the popular author Richard Bach, "You are never given a dream without also being given the power to make it true. You may have to work for it, however." You are not just a laborer, teacher, usher, choir member, doctor, lawyer, college student, veterinarian, mother, sister, brother, husband, or wife. You are more. You are the redeemed, regenerated, born-again seed of God who has been given dominion on earth. You are capable of overcoming and able to overcome every obstacle or crisis placed in your life!

"And we know that God causes everything to work together for the good of those who love God and are called according to his purpose for them. For God knew his people in advance, and he chose them to become like his Son, so that his Son would be the firstborn among many brothers and sisters." (Romans 8:28-29)

We know that God's plan is the best plan because he is the beginning and the end. He has already seen the end of your life and has known you from the beginning. The Word of God is full of his promises of blessing for us. Did you know that God wants you blessed, prosperous, and healed? He wants you supplied with all good things. One day while I was praying about some of my life's concerns, Holy Spirit spoke to me and said to trust in his goodness and his plan. This put my mind and spirit at rest. God doesn't want us overly concerned about anything. He has a plan and wants us to wholeheartedly trust him. Read Matthew 6:31-32 to cast worry out of your spirit!

Claim the real you today by embracing the Father's plan for your life. Ask yourself this question: Is God's plan for my life worth going after? Of course it is! Here are some things to do and keep in mind as you seek God's plan and purpose for your life.

1. **Say this prayer confession daily**:

   Father, thank you for the power to become your child through Christ. Lord, I thank you for the plan and purpose that you have for my life. I know your plan is good. I trust you and receive your plan for my life by faith. I am trusting in your goodness. Thank you, Father, for ordering my steps in your plan.

2. **Daily seek God's face to know who you are—the real you.**

   You don't have to beg and plead with the Father to show you his plan. He wants to show you, although he may not show you his entire plan at one time.

3. **Meditate on these Scriptures as well as the other Power Scriptures throughout this book:**

   Jeremiah 29:11, Proverbs 3:5-6, and Romans 8:27-28. When you meditate on something, you think about it over and over. You say it to yourself quietly or aloud until it is embedded in your mind and heart.

I remember this being how our little girl studied her vowel sounds. She said them over and over until she was saying them in her sleep. It was the sweetest thing ever to see. You need to treat Scripture the same way. Meditate upon it until its truth is rooted in your heart. Meditation changes your thinking.

4. **Keep an open mind when God speaks to you.**

Trust him even though what he tells you may not seem possible in your mind. When God told me that I was a pastor and a preacher, it was hard for me to receive because I had a past that I was not proud of. But that did not negate the Father's plan for me.

5. **Be obedient to God's voice and do what he tells you to do, even when you don't see a benefit to doing so.**

The Father knows what he is doing. The Bible tells us that if we are willing and obedient, we shall eat the good of the land. (Isaiah 1:18-20)

For example, after prayer one morning, the Lord spoke to me and told me that he wanted me to start going to the nursing homes within the city and singing to and praying for the elderly. Being young in the Lord, I immediately called my pastor because I felt I needed further guidance. Once I got my pastor on the phone, he said, "That sounds like God. Go!" In my mind, I was wondering why in the world God would send me to the nursing home. That's not really my forté. However, I obeyed His will faithfully. At first, I was afraid and actually trembled when I started to sing, but after a while I gained confidence and before long, I was singing, praying, and reading Scriptures to the elderly residents.

Obedience is one thing. Actually, bringing your heart and mind in line with God's is another.

Obedience is one thing. Actually, bringing your heart and mind in line with God's is another. I remember one incident in particular that changed the way I looked at my walk with God. It was a sunny afternoon, and I went to make my rounds of praying, singing, and witnessing at the nursing home. I came to the room of an elderly woman who had some of her limbs amputated due to diabetes. When I arrived in her doorway, Holy Spirit led me to pray for her, so I did. When I finished, it was as if the Lord took over my being and spoke through me and said, "I just wanted to come see about you." The woman just cried and cried. It was amazing. God had used me—little, nothing me—to show this woman that he cared for her and she was not forgotten. This encouraged me even more to walk in obedience, coupled with seeing many elderly people accept Christ as their Lord and Savior.

When you submit to God and allow him to use you, your perspective changes and great things happen.

You start to understand that God loves us no matter what condition or stage of life we are in. You start to realize what is important in life—loving and helping other people and going beyond yourself as Jesus did to help us.

6. **Trust God's plan for your life daily regardless of difficult circumstances you are facing.**

   The Father wants the best for you. Whether it is the need for healing in your physical body, financial freedom, or deliverance from drug addiction, fear, and guilt, you will soon find that as you seek the Father and understand your relationship with him, you will discover the deep treasure of inheritance he has already given you to fulfill his plan.

Empowerment Tools

Write down five things you want to do in your life or those things you believe God has spoken to you. When making your list, be bold and honest in what you want and believe:

1.

2.

3.

4.

5.

God wants to give you good things. Ask him to align your will with his so you receive his best.

Power Scriptures

Romans 8:28

And we know that God causes everything to work together for the good of those who love God and are called according to his purpose for them.

John 16:23

At that time you won't need to ask me for anything. I tell you the truth, you will ask the Father directly, and he will grant your request because you use my name.

Psalm 138:8

The Lord will work out his plans for my life— for your faithful love, O Lord, endures forever. Don't abandon me, for you made me.

Chapter 5

Breaking Free from the Past

I remember crying my eyes out and curling up in the fetal position in my little red Ford Tempo outside of an office building of a psychiatrist I was waiting to see. It was as though the world was caving in on me. I was so depressed. I felt so defeated.

I had recently filed for a divorce in my one-week marriage, and I had lost my job. Every decision I had made seemed to be the wrong one. My life was falling apart, and so was I. Hurt had piled upon hurt, and all my efforts seemed to be no more than Band-Aids on my emotional and spiritual wounds. (As a pastor, I see many young women doing the same things.) They get out of one hurtful or abusive relationship only to quickly jump into another. One bad decision follows another, yet somehow, they think that they can continue this pattern and have a positive end.

After I saw the psychiatrist, I felt even more defeated. She proceeded to tell me I was very depressed. I already knew this and didn't have money or health insurance to get treated, so I left.

I drove to my apartment, where I lived with my two unsaved sisters (at that time) and informed one of them that I was losing my mind. Her reply was, "You are not losing your mind. Get out of my room!"

I ran frantically to my bedroom, where I could feel my mind and ability to speak slowly slip from me. The feeling was indescribable. I felt so helpless. All my thoughts were draining away, and my awareness was drifting. I felt Holy Spirit rise up in me and say, "fight." So, I began to call on the name of Jesus. With my last piece of mind and weak voice, I uttered these words, "Jesus, heal my mind." Suddenly, I could speak, and I felt my mind being restored back to me. Hallelujah!

From that day on, I began fighting for my life spiritually and learning of the power I had through Christ. You see, I was born again but ignorant of the power within me until Holy Spirit showed me that it was there. You have that same power to receive healing and get a turnaround in your life. You have been brought into right relationship with the Father, and you have what the Father has FOR YOU because of Jesus.

Break the Chains!

Perhaps you have an awful past. Perhaps you have made mistakes from which you feel you cannot recover. Don't allow the demons of your past to keep you in bondage and away from your heavenly Father. Don't walk around depressed and defeated. All things are possible with God (Matthew 19:26). The Father loves you unconditionally. He doesn't care that you were born out of wedlock or that you come from a dysfunctional family. He doesn't care that you were once promiscuous or that you did something that landed you in a prison cell. He has big plans for you, but you have to want to be a part of them.

There is an old African proverb that says, "If there is no enemy within, the enemy outside can't harm us." You see, it is the way we view ourselves (past hurts, inward struggles, and self-rejection) that keeps us from becoming all God wants us to be. I'm not saying that your past was not painful or that your current situation is not a reality—but you can be free today by faith.

I'm not saying that your past was not painful or that your current situation is not a reality—but you can be free today by faith.

When my husband and I got married over twenty-one years ago, he had three beautiful daughters and one son, ages eight, eleven, thirteen and seventeen. They had experienced the traumatic effects of divorce. This was very difficult for us. I did not have children yet and had not experienced real married life before. I was single for most of my young adult life (married only one week in the past) and very business oriented and independent. I had come from a dysfunctional family as well. Although there were other outside forces that make stepparenting difficult, which I won't mention in this book, I knew there was something deeper on the inside of me that kept me from giving them my all. Although I loved them, it was difficult for me to fully show that love.

Although I wanted to embrace them more, I struggled with the spirit of rejection because I had experienced the effects of rejection when my father left. I was fearful that they would not accept me.

Joyce Meyer wrote a powerful book called *The Root of Rejection*. In it she writes, "The word rejection means to be cast aside; to be thrown away as having no value. To be rejected means being told 'I don't want you—you have no value!' When that happens to a person, it is very painful. God did not create us to be rejected. He created us to be accepted, loved, and valued. There is nothing in our God-given nature that can accept being rejected."[2]

It was not until I tapped into my inheritance that my life was healed. I discovered that I possessed all the power to give and receive love in all my relationships.

Through much prayer, Father God showed me the root of the stronghold while I was reading this Scripture: "But as many as received him, to them gave he power to become the sons of God, even to them that believe on his name" (John 1:12). As I read, the Lord showed me that I was His and that I had been given power, meaning the privilege to be called his own and belonging to his family. He showed me that I mattered, that I was valuable to him (as well as others), and that whatever I needed was mine through Christ.

I began to seek God. Through prayer and worship, I was able to pull down my inheritance of healing. It had never dawned on me that I needed healing in this way. Through this revealing, God healed me, and I came into the renewed understanding. I now knew that I possessed his true power to love and forgive. I was delivered from the spirit of rejection, selfishness, shame, and fear. You see, I had to face the enemy within me—my past hurts.

I was delivered from the spirit of rejection, selfishness, shame, and fear. You see, I had to face the enemy within me—my past hurts.

I cannot tell you how much they (my children) have enriched and blessed my life. I welcome and adore what the Father has given me in all my children and grandchildren. My life is full of love now. We have grown together so much!

I can truly say that I am enjoying this blessed life the Father has given us together in all his wisdom and knowledge. We are a truly loving and blended family.

I pray that, as you come into the revelation that you have full acceptance in the Father, you will learn what I did—that anyone who has accepted Jesus has become a new creation. The old things have passed away and everything has become new. From this point on, believe by faith that God has forgiven and healed you, even though you may not feel like it at this point. Keep confessing by faith and you'll soon see your healing manifest.

Empowerment Tools

List five things from the past that hurt you or any inward struggles, demonic strongholds, or unforgiveness that seem immovable. Give each to God in prayer. It is okay if you are still angry. This isn't something you have to try to hide from God. He knows this already.

1.

2.

3.

4.

5.

Now that you have made your list, give the things you listed over to God in prayer. Pray this:

Father, I release my past today. I thank you that my past is covered by the shed blood of Jesus Christ. I receive your Word that I am healed according to Isaiah 53:5. I forgive myself and others for my past mistakes, failures, and negative experiences.

Power Scriptures

2 Corinthians 5:17

This means that anyone who belongs to Christ has become a new person. The old life is gone; a new life has begun!

Isaiah 53:5

But he was pierced for our rebellion, crushed for our sins. He was beaten so we could be whole. He was whipped so we could be healed.

Chapter 6

No Longer Slaves, but Sons

But as many as received him, to them gave he power to become the sons of God, even to them that believe on his name." (John 1:12 KJV)

According to the Word of God, we have been given the power (which means the right and privilege) to become sons of God as soon as we receive Jesus Christ. As you grow in Christ and in his love, you become fully aware of what belongs to you as a one of his children. You will no longer walk in fear but in power and confidence as a son (male or female).

"Such love has no fear because perfect love expels all fear. If we are afraid, it is for fear of punishment, and this shows that we have not fully experienced his perfect love." (1 John 4:18)

A son who has a good and faithful father and a real relationship with his father does not walk in fear of him, even when he makes a mistake. He realizes that his father loves him no matter what. As he matures, his father begins to entrust his son with more responsibility. As the child grows, his father will trust him with even more.

No matter where you are in your journey with Christ, whether this revelation is new or something you have struggled to embrace for some time, God is showing you around the kingdom. Holy Spirit is your guide. Just as an earthly father is anxious to show his son around his earthly inheritance, the Father is showing you the many rooms of blessing and riches in his kingdom. You see, you not only need what the Father has, but you have it already. According to Ephesians 1:3, you are already seated in heavenly places with him. All you need to do is know through his Word that you possess all things and confess his Word in faith to see those riches manifest in your life.

You are filled with untapped potential. Forget about your past and start reaching for your future. You have a newfound relationship with your Father. Embrace it!

Why We Don't Receive

As a pastor, I have seen people come to the altar in the spirit of condemnation, and even though part of our inheritance is full acceptance in Christ, still live in the spirit of condemnation. What a shame! Condemnation means a person is "pronounced to be wrong, guilty, worthless, or forfeited; adjudged or sentenced to punishment, destruction, or useless and fit only for destruction."

When a person walks in condemnation and fear, it hinders them from asking and receiving from the

Father in faith and confidence what they need or desire. For example, we are less apt to ask a person we don't know or trust for something than one we do know or trust. This is not just because of the fear that they won't give us what we ask for, but fear that they will reject us completely. It breaks my heart to see the loved, cherished children of God do this, especially when I know that God has already forgiven them. They just cannot overcome the wrong they have done. Perhaps they slipped back into a fornicating relationship, had a baby out of wedlock, committed robbery, or continue to struggle with the guilt and shame of being a victim of rape or abuse. They cannot see themselves as victorious or righteous. They are blinded by darkness because their eyes are closed to the truth of the reconciliation and forgiveness provided for them through Christ.

You are not enslaved to the bondage of fear but free in the love of Christ.

"For God made Christ, who never sinned, to be the offering for our sin, so that we could be made right with God through Christ." (2 Corinthians 5:21 NLT)

When we view ourselves as condemned, we walk in fear. This is a spirit from the devil. When we see ourselves this way, we are not yet mature in Christ's love for us. As we grow in Christ, he gives us more responsibility. He can trust us to faithfully fulfill His purpose. It is difficult to trust a child who has not fully grown into an adult or come into maturity. He or she does not know how to handle such responsibility. Just as a child must sincerely desire to learn from his earthly father and earn his trust, so believers must desire the sincere milk of the Word of God so we can grow and mature and know how to discern what is good and what is evil. The Father has given us grace to do so.

You are made righteous through Christ, so start seeing yourself that way. Grow in spiritual stature and favor as Jesus did when he was a child. The Holy Spirit of God is in you, bringing you into the blessedness of Christ and transforming you into the image of Christ. Stop walking in fear. You may have heard that God is a consuming fire, but God is also a forgiving God of love, and he is your heavenly Father. So, stand firm in his love.

"For [the Spirit which] you have now received [is] not a spirit of slavery to put you once more in bondage to fear, but you have received the Spirit of adoption [the Spirit producing sonship] in [the bliss of] which we cry, Abba (Father)! Father! The Spirit Himself [thus] testifies together with our own spirit, [assuring us] that we are children of God." (Romans 8:15-16 AMP)

Trust the Father to mature you in his perfect love. Let me say this again. Trust the Father to mature you in his perfect love. My prayer for you today is that God the Father will draw you closer with his love and kindness so you may start to live and operate in the power he has granted you through receiving Jesus Christ.

Praying in Power

When we understand our relationship to the Father and what Christ has done for us, we begin to pray from a different position. We no longer pray from the position of servant to master but as a son to a Father in faith of His Word. I believe this is the position in which the Father says, "Ask for whatever you want and it shall be given unto you." Glory to God!

We no longer pray as beggars but as believers that he is the Father and desires to give us what we ask in faith.

One Wednesday night, I was leading prayer at church. As I began to pray, I noticed that my prayer was different this time. As I walked back to my seat, the Lord revealed to me that it felt different because I had prayed from a different position. I had come into the revelation and boldness that he is my Father and that with that revelation, I can ask the Father anything in Jesus' name in faith and confidence and he will answer me.

If we are sons (male or female) of the Father, why don't our prayers always get answered? I believe it is because we pray from the wrong position. We pray from the point of view that we do not have the right to ask for what we need or want. We come with the attitude, "God, we beg you," and offer "If you would be so kind, sir" types of prayers. In doing so, we pray from the position of a stranger rather than the position of a son. Stop praying from the wrong position. As believers, we have been uniquely positioned in the heavenly places with Christ Jesus, who says:

"At that time you will ask (pray) in My Name; and I am not saying that I will ask the Father on your behalf [for it will be unnecessary]. For the Father Himself [tenderly] loves you because you have loved Me and have believed that I came out from the Father." (John 16:26-27 AMP)

That is awesome! In paraphrasing those verses above, Jesus said that once he returned to the Father, we could pray to the Father ourselves in his name because the Father loves us.

Nor do we have to beg God for what he has already given us. We just need to ask in faith.

We don't understand the power in His name, and we often do not pray from a position of heirship in which we are seated in heavenly places (Ephesians 2:6), blood-washed and delivered from the curse. Instead of coming in faith to the Father as Christ did, realizing that we are his and he is ours and presenting all that Christ is, we come in unbelief, fear, and as strangers. We end our doubt-filled prayers with "In Jesus' name," and nothing happens. Needless to say, we become discouraged. We do not have to be. Nor do we have to beg God for what he has already given us. We just need to ask in faith.

"In Jesus' Name"

With that said, what does it really mean when we say, "In Jesus' name"? It means to have faith in the power and authority of Jesus Christ given to him by the Father that we now possess as joint heirs. It means to pray to the Father by presenting all that Christ is and has done. Each time we declare his name to the Father, we do so with the realization, understanding, and knowledge of the power available to us in Christ, in whom the fullness of the Godhead dwells and who is the head of all principality and power. (Col. 2:9-10)

As we develop our relationship with the Father, we become more enlightened about what Jesus has done for us in bringing us into fellowship with the Father. Remember that part of your inheritance through Christ is power and authority. From now on, understand your position and supernatural ability in Christ to speak to mountains and have them move, lay hands on the sick and see them recover, and cast out demonic spirits.

By faith God has already given us what we need. He is not standing there, holding blessings over our heads that he doesn't want to give us. Scripture says that if he freely gave his only begotten Son, how much more will he give us everything else? Reading and meditating on this Scripture will increase your faith and strengthen your confidence as you pray. Faith comes by hearing the

Word of God. All we need to do is supply the faith and then access what the Father has for us, whether it is salvation, healing, prosperity, understanding, or our life's purpose.

Empowerment Tools

List five things that you desire to do but have not done in your life, ministry, business, or relationships because of fear. These things can be ideas, inventions, or business endeavors you had but didn't pursue because you were afraid of what people might think or because you felt your ideas weren't good enough or that you weren't qualified to pursue them.

1.

2.

3.

4.

5.

Now confront your fears with the Word of God, which says, "For God did not give us a spirit of timidity (of cowardice, of craven and cringing and fawning fear), but [He has given us a spirit] of power and of love and of calm and well-balanced mind and discipline and self-control." (2 Timothy 1:7 AMP)

Power Scripture

2 Timothy 1:7 (NLT)

For God has not given us a spirit of fear and timidity, but of power, love, and self-discipline.

Chapter 7

Fearless Confidence

Some time ago, I was doing marketing for a successful relocation company that had several offices throughout the United States. The company was privately held and the owner had two children who worked at the company as well. I would often notice how the owner's daughter would walk around the company in confidence. She knew she did not have to worry about not having a job or being late. She drove the best cars and wore the most beautiful clothes. She was always kind and confident. She would affectionately interact with her father. She held her head up high. She had a relationship with her father and knew he would take care of her. She knew she had special privileges. She knew she could trust him.

"Those who know their fathers are confident. They know if all fails, they have someone they can depend on or have a strong shoulder to cry on. They don't walk around with their heads sunk down, barely getting by. In the kingdom of God, the Bible says that they who know their God shall do exploits." (Daniel 11:32 AMP) Too many of us do not know the Father. Therefore, we are not confident in his ability or that he will give us what we ask for. We don't interact with him affectionately nor rest in him when we have a problem. When we do not receive what we ask for, we carry needless burdens on our shoulders and stay mad at the world and God. We don't understand how we can be saved, live "right," and go to church every Sunday, but still not have what the Father has given us through Christ. We become angry and distant from him. We give up, and it's all because we have not developed our relationship to know beyond a shadow of a doubt that he has given us all things through Christ.

One night after one of our ministry revivals, there were several people standing around after church. It was late and our little girl, who was six years old at the time, slowly climbed into the arms of my husband. Eventually she fell asleep, and her little neck went limp as she rested. She looked so comfortable. She was confident that she would be safe in his arms and that he would not let any harm come to her. She could completely let go and sleep in the presence of strangers because he would protect her. That is how the Father wants us to be. He wants us to trust him so much that we are not afraid to crawl into his arms and enter his rest, knowing that he is working on all of our concerns. This trust and rest only come by relationship, knowing that he loves us and is genuinely concerned about us.

"In this [union and communion with Him] love is brought to completion and attains perfection with us, that we may have confidence for the day of judgment [with assurance and boldness to face Him], because as He is, so are we in this world." (1 John 4:17 AMP)

How do you gain this same confidence? Spend time with the Father. When you do, you will get to know him. You will learn his love for you, what belongs to you and his perfect will for you. We have a rich inheritance through Christ Jesus. So, make time with the Father your priority. When you spend time in prayer, don't turn it into a begging session. Go confidently to the Father in faith and make your requests known unto him. Then wait patiently for its manifestation.

Rid yourself of all insecurity. When we are insecure, we are unstable in the love of our heavenly Father. We doubt his care and concern for us. The love of the Father is unconditional. It is not based on how good we are but on how good he is. Insecurity causes feelings of rejection and the need to please others. As a result, I believe both our relationships with others and with our heavenly Father suffer greatly.

Look at it this way. When children come home, they enter with confidence and assurance. They walk in and get what they want to eat or drink out of the refrigerator, plop down on the couch, turn on the television, and relax. They are confident that what belongs to their parents belongs to them. Particularly if they have loving parents, they are confident that the love their parents have for them has not changed because of their past behavior. There may be chastisement, but their parents' love remains. This is the frame of mind we should have as God's dear children. We should be confident that what our Father has belongs to us because of Christ Jesus.

Settle In

Another way to strengthen your confidence so that you may possess God's promises in your life is to understand the concept of adoption in Christ. We are adopted into his family. What would happen if you were to adopt a child?

Would you expect that child to act any differently than your other children? Of course not! That child is now yours, fully accepted. You would expect them to come in and join in the family activities, traditions, chores, prayers, and wealth just as your other children. That might be hard for the newly adopted child to accept, but it's true, nonetheless. It might be very different from what they are used to. Perhaps they came from families where there was a lot of fear, rejection, or insecurity. It might take a while to realize and accept what it means to have full membership in your family, but after a while, they will embrace their new relationship, their new inheritance, and they will settle in.

After I left my job at a prominent company in Memphis, Tennessee, the Holy Spirit spoke to me, and that is exactly what he said: "Settle in." He wanted me to learn to settle into a new system—his system, his way of doing things, his way of providing for and blessing me. This would not be easy. I was used to a paycheck on a regular basis. I had settled for the world system providing for me, and as a result, I lived from paycheck to paycheck. I had made my job my source, even though this was not my intention from the beginning.

To "settle in" means to snuggle down, park ourselves, to become accustomed to, or familiarize ourselves with something. In this case, we should settle in with kingdom living. We are so accustomed to operating by the standards and dictates of the world that we miss out on the blessedness that comes from living as part of the kingdom of God.

"By his divine power, God has given us everything we need for living a godly life. We have received all of this by coming to know him, the one who called us to himself by means of his marvelous glory and excellence." (2 Peter 1:3)

We are to have dominion on earth by being God's ambassadors, fulfilling our God-given purpose and being victorious. God has given us power and authority to prevail over every evil and hindrance on this earth. When Jesus returns, he wants us to have accomplished our tasks.

Child of God, you have what it takes already on the inside of you, even if you don't realize it now. When we become desperate enough, we will seek the kingdom of God. In this, we should be just like the woman in the Bible who lost one of her silver pieces. In this story, the woman lost a precious silver coin and tore up her house to find it. I encourage you to have this same hunger for receiving what the Father has for us. Settle into the kingdom life and find out your purpose, then God will meet your every need.

It's Your Inheritance—Claim It!

In "settling in" and receiving what the Father has for you, be like the daughters of Zelophehad. I refer to them as the "fearless five" because they stood before Moses, Eleazar, the priest, the leaders, and all the congregation and demanded their inheritance. They knew their father had given them something and they wanted it.

Then came the daughters of Zelophehad, the son of Hepher, the son of Gilead, the son of Machir, the son of Manasseh, from the families of Manasseh the son of Joseph; and these were the names of his daughters: Mahlah, Noah, Hoglah, Milcah, and Tirzah. [2] And they stood before Moses, before Eleazar the priest, and before the leaders and all the congregation, by the doorway of the tabernacle of meeting, saying: [3] "Our father died in the wilderness; but he was not in the company of those who gathered together against the Lord, in company with Korah, but he died in his own sin; and he had no sons. [4] Why should the name of our father be removed from among his family because he had no son? Give us a possession among our father's brothers." [5] So Moses brought their case before the Lord. [6] And the Lord spoke to Moses, saying: "The daughters of Zelophehad speak what is right; you shall surely give them a possession of inheritance among their father's brothers, and cause the inheritance of their father to pass to them. (Numbers 27:1-6)

These daughters did not care what people thought. They did not care that it was tradition and law. The law stated that if a father died, the inheritance would be passed on to his sons. If he had no sons, it would be passed on to his brothers. This totally left these women without an inheritance, and that was not something they would accept.

Be bold and confident in what the Father has done for you in Christ. He wants you to have your inheritance. It gives him pleasure to see you blessed and fulfilling your purpose in life. Because these daughters challenged the law, the law was changed: "And you shall speak to the children of Israel, saying: 'If a man dies and has no son, then you shall cause his inheritance to pass to his daughter.'" (Numbers 27:8 NKJV)

Don't allow tradition or the fact that something has never been done before stop you. Have the audacity to believe God. If he says that you are to preach, then preach. If God tells you to start a business, start it. If he tells you that you have the gift of healing by the laying on of hands, then receive it and operate!

Even after Moses' death, the daughters of Zelophehad appeared before Joshua as he gave out allotment. They reminded him of God's command. Consequently, Joshua gave them their inheritance. Receive yours!

Empowerment Tools

List three things that you can go after with fearless confidence now! This can be your healing, financial freedom, job, or deliverance! Write it down and decree that you have what the Father has for you!

1.

2.

3.

4.

5.

Power Scriptures

1 John 3:21

Dear friends, if we don't feel guilty, we can come to God with bold confidence.

Hebrews 10:35

So do not throw away this confident trust in the Lord. Remember the great reward it brings you!

Chapter 8

Reunited With the Father

It is a wise father who knows his child. But maybe it's a very wise child who takes time to know his father. — Anonymous

Jesus came to bring us back into fellowship with the Father. But what does being reunited with your heavenly Father really mean? When Jesus died on the cross for us, he redeemed us from the curse of the law (Galatians 4:5-6). He came to introduce us back to our heavenly Father. It was God's plan to bring us back to him—and he did. God loved us so much that he gave his only begotten son, Jesus Christ. It is God's desire that we know him.

Imagine being reunited with your rich father whom you have not seen or known in years. Imagine he is richer than Jeff Bezos and Bill Gates put together. Imagine that he desires a relationship with you and wants to give you the desires of your heart. He wants to catch up on all he has missed in your life. He wants to protect you and provide for you. All you have to do is receive him and let him know that you want a relationship with him, then passionately work to build that relationship.

I have at least an inkling of what this is like. After almost twenty-five years, my father came back into my life and desired a relationship with me, my sisters, and my brothers. I had to choose to receive him and get to know him. This took effort. I really didn't see what we had in common. I didn't have good memories of him. Picking out a Father's Day card was difficult because one full of accolades and memories did not apply. In order to develop our relationship, I had to work at it. I had to call him and accept the calls he made to me. Although we were miles apart, we chose to visit, spend time together, send text messages, and interact. I had to accept or receive the relationship just as you must accept and receive what Jesus has done for you in bringing you into fellowship with the Father.

"But to as many as did receive and welcome Him, He gave the authority (power, privilege, right) to become the children of God, that is, to those who believe in (adhere to, trust in, and rely on) His name—Who owe their birth neither to bloods nor to the will of the flesh [that of physical impulse] nor to the will of man [that of a natural father], but to God. [They are born of God!]" (John 1:12-13 AMP)

God has given us the power and right to become his children. Think on this. Through Christ you now have the power and privilege to come to God as your Father. One night while reading the above passage of Scripture, the Holy Spirit asked me, "What is a Father?" I had never been asked that question before. Nor, for that matter, had I even thought about it. More importantly, I was surprised when I could not answer the question without guessing. At that moment, I realized that I had no real concept of what a good father was like. I began to cry uncontrollably.

God showed me that he was a good father. Because my father had been absent most of my life, I never understood what a good father was or should be. Without a real earthly example, there was a big blank in my mind. As I searched inwardly, I found that my understanding of a father was someone upon whom I could not depend. To me, a father was someone who was not present when I needed him the most, someone who had abandoned me as a young girl, and who was not there for me now. A father was someone who never told me he was proud of me. He was not someone I could trust.

From my understanding of an earthly father, I had built an attitude of self-reliance and an iron heart. I was, however, overwhelmed that God loved me and had grafted me into his family and that he was a father upon whom I could depend. He was one who would protect me. I had made so many mistakes, done so many things I was not proud of, and yet he loves me unconditionally. He will never leave me nor forsake me. That is who my Father is! Even believers who have been saved for years and attend church faithfully often operate without a real relationship—this kind of relationship—with the Father.

Jesus showed us the glory and the blessing of a relationship with the Father. Jesus did miracles, including turning water to wine, raising the dead, and healing the sick. He was our example of what we can accomplish when we have a true relationship with the Father through him. The Father, the Son, and the Holy Spirit are one, and we are one with the Father through Christ.

"And you are in Him, made full and having come to fullness of life [in Christ you too are filled with the Godhead—Father, Son and Holy Spirit—and reach full spiritual stature]. And He is the Head of all rule and authority [of every angelic principality and power]." (Colossians 2:10 AMP)

To have what the Father has, we have to receive what Jesus has done for us. When I say, "receive him," I mean to accept, acknowledge, trust, and have faith. Just because God has given or provided something for us, his children, does not mean that we will obtain it. God gave his only begotten Son for all, but many still have not received him as their personal Savior. God has given us healing through the stripes of Jesus Christ, yet we walk around sick. God has brought us into right relationship through the death, burial, and resurrection of Jesus Christ, but we continue to live lives of defeat, rejection, and uncertainty. If God is our Father, why should we fear?

If we are not careful, we will allow disappointment, lack of knowledge, and circumstances to keep us from a true experience and relationship with God. I want to encourage you to open your heart and allow God to heal you of every hurt and pain. Get on your knees and get into his presence. He's waiting. Remember, child of God, he has so much for you, and you can have what the Father has for you by getting to know him. Your relationship has already been set up. It's like a blind date. You may have never met, but a good friend whom you know and trust thought you were a great match. All you have to do is meet, and the relationship could lead to something much more, like marriage. Jesus has already brought you to the Father by his precious blood. To receive and know him, all you have to do is develop that relationship through Christ with prayer, worship, praise, and a heart of acceptance and gratitude.

Perhaps this understanding of God as Father is something you've heard before. Perhaps you once had a relationship with the Father, but through long periods of delays and disappointments, that relationship has suffered.

Maybe you feel distant from God, and all of this talk about "having what the Father has" is painful because you once had that relationship, but now it is gone. I want to encourage you to open your heart again and receive the love of God anew. Embrace his sweet assurance. He is still there for you. The Christian author Robin Jones Gunn once said, "If you feel far from God, guess who moved?" It's not God! He's there, arms outstretched like the father of the prodigal son, waiting for you to come back.

Does It Really Matter?

As I stated earlier, my biological father came back into my life when I was almost thirty years old. This relationship was still relevant and important to my life, although it took me a while to see it. My initial thought was to reject him because of past pain. I could think of a thousand reasons why I should. It's too late, I thought. I'm too old; he hurt me; I don't need him now; I can make it without him; and on and on. I had set my heart to live without him. Have you set your heart to live without God due to life's disappointments?

However, as we renewed and developed our relationship, something in me began to change. I felt a part of him. I felt a sense of belonging. Week by week, month by month, and year by year, we spoke over the phone, visited, and attended church services together. Today, I am closer to my father than I have ever been, and I love him. I admire his newfound love in our heavenly Father and freedom in Christ. I honor my Father in words and deeds and I am here for him. I also see his humanness and vulnerability. I genuinely care for my dad, and our relationship is important to me.

One day, I informed my dad that my real estate business was growing and prospering. He put his hand on my shoulder and said, "I'm proud of you, sweetheart." That day, something in me changed. Something in me was healed and rewarded. Something in me was restored. I felt valued, accepted, and empowered. My father said he was proud of me. I had nothing more to prove to anyone. That battle inside me was put to rest. What needs to be put to rest in your life? That night, I cried. I had never before heard my father tell me that he was proud of me. His words were so important to me. They gave me confidence. A father should speak good things and blessings over his children just as the Father has spoken blessings over us. One word from your heavenly Father can change your life and make you whole. Holy Spirit will declare the Father's words for you—to you—through his Spirit and the Word of God. There is power in the mouth of our earthly fathers, and there is even more power in the mouth of our heavenly Father. Our heavenly Father has spoken blessings over us.

It's All There

Everything you need is in the Father's house, meaning the kingdom of God in you. It's your right and privilege to come boldly and receive it. Don't worry about your shortcomings or your circumstances. Move by faith to receive the rich treasures your heavenly Father has for you today.

"Since he did not spare even his own Son but gave him up for us all, won't he also give us everything else?" (Romans 8:32)

My prayer for you is that you will claim your inheritance as a child of the Most High God. I pray that you will obtain all that the Father has for you as you seek his face and receive understanding of your purpose, his will, and your inheritance. I pray for a new day in your life and that the fragrance of God's presence will overtake every situation and difficult circumstance that you are facing. I pray that you will live a life of victory, child of God, knowing that you already have what the Father has for you!

Empowerment Tools

Name five steps you will take to develop a closer relationship with Father God.

1.

2.

3.

4.

5.

Power Scriptures

Ephesians 1:3

All praise to God, the Father of our Lord Jesus Christ, who has blessed us with every spiritual blessing in the heavenly realms because we are united with Christ.

Ephesians 2:13

But now you have been united with Christ Jesus. Once you were far away from God, but now you have been brought near to him through the blood of Christ.

Ephesians 2:14

For Christ himself has brought peace to us. He united Jews and Gentiles into one people when, in his own body on the cross, he broke down the wall of hostility that separated us.

The Sinner's Prayer

In this book we have talked about many promises and principles from God's precious Word. Even if you are not yet adopted into God's family, the good news is that this gift is for everyone, no matter who you are or what background you are from.

"For God loved the world so much that he gave his one and only Son, so that everyone who believes in him will not perish but have eternal life." (John 3:16)

If you are not yet part of this family, I want to invite you to be part of the family of God by accepting Jesus Christ as your Lord and Savior today. All you need to do is believe in your heart what Jesus has done according to the Word of God and confess that belief with your mouth. When you do, you become a part of God's family. You are now saved.

If you confess with your mouth that Jesus is Lord and believe in your heart that God raised him from the dead, you will be saved. For it is by believing in your heart that you are made right with God, and it is by confessing with your mouth that you are saved. (Rom. 10:9-10)

If you would like to be part of God's family, please say this prayer below:

Heavenly Father, I believe that Jesus Christ is the Son of the living God and that he died on the cross so that I may have forgiveness for my sins and eternal life. I know that without you in my heart, my life is meaningless. I believe that you raised Jesus Christ from the dead. Please forgive me for every sin in my life. I accept your son, Jesus Christ, into my heart. I need you to be my Father and my friend. I give you my life and ask you to take full control from this moment on. I pray this in the name of Jesus Christ. Amen.

Now confess this: *I am now saved!*

Congratulations! Welcome to the family of God and to all the inheritance God your Father has for you!

Endnotes

1. Napoleon Hill, *Think and Grow Rich* (New York: Random House), p. 38, p.42

2. Joyce Meyer, *The Root of Rejection* (Tulsa, OK: Harrison House, 1965, 1987), pp. 41-42

About the Author

Lydia J. Nance is an ordained minister at Philadelphia Outreach Ministries in West Memphis, Arkansas, where she passionately and faithfully co-pastors with her husband, Dr. Steven Nance, Sr. Pastor, teaching and preaching the Word of God.

They have been married for twenty-two years and have five beautiful children and several grandchildren.

She has a love for the work of God where she counsels, exhorts, and empowers the people of God. She has been in ministry for over twenty-five years.

She was born and raised in Niagara Falls, New York. After the death of her mother, she moved from New York to Memphis, Tennessee, where she attended and graduated from the University of Memphis, receiving her Bachelor of Art degree in journalism. She has a passion for writing, mentoring, serving, and teaching the Word of God.

Additionally, Nance is an author, songwriter, licensed

Real Estate Broker, investor, and entrepreneur.

She loves to write, travel, refurbish furniture (in her spare time) and drink coffee and spend time with her family.

We would love to hear your testimony on how this book has ministered and helped you.

Please write to:

Philadelphia Ministries, Inc. 407 Birch Street

West Memphis, AR 72301

Email: *lydiancebooks@gmail.com*

YOU HAVE WHAT THE *Father* HAS

Made in the USA
Monee, IL
04 November 2026

67391350R10066